T0055495

PRESENTED TO:

FROM:

DATE:

THE ENNEAGRAM COLLECTION

THE LOYAL GUARDIAN

6

ENNEAGRAM TYPE

BETH McCORD

Your **Enneagram** Coach

THOMAS NELSON

Since 1798

Enneagram Type 6: The Loyal Guardian

© 2019 by Beth McCord

All rights reserved. No portion of this book may be reproduced, stored in a retrieval system, or transmitted in any form or by any means—electronic, mechanical, photocopy, recording, scanning, or other—except for brief quotations in critical reviews or articles, without the prior written permission of the publisher.

Published in Nashville, Tennessee, by Thomas Nelson. Thomas Nelson is a registered trademark of HarperCollins Christian Publishing, Inc.

Published in association with Alive Literary Agency.

Unless otherwise noted, Scripture quotations are taken from the ESV® Bible (The Holy Bible, English Standard Version®), copyright © 2001 by Crossway, a publishing ministry of Good News Publishers. Used by permission. All rights reserved.

Any Internet addresses, phone numbers, or company or product information printed in this book are offered as a resource and are not intended in any way to be or to imply an endorsement by Thomas Nelson, nor does Thomas Nelson vouch for the existence, content, or services of these sites, phone numbers, companies, or products beyond the life of this book.

Graphic Designer: Jane Butler, Well Refined Creative Director, wellrefined.co
Interior Designer: Emily Ghattas
Cover Designer: Greg Jackson at Thinkpen Design

ISBN 978-1-4002-1795-3 (audiobook)
ISBN 978-1-4002-1937-7 (eBook)
ISBN 978-1-4002-1570-6 (HC)

Printed in Malaysia

23 24 25 26 27 OFF 7 6 5 4 3

Contents

Foreword V

Introduction IX

Overview of the Nine Enneagram Types 1

Overview of Type 6: The Loyal Guardian 9

Day 1: Faith and the Enneagram 13

Day 2: Being Aware 21

Day 3: Core Motivations 27

Day 4: Core Fear 33

Day 5: Core Desire 39

Day 6: Core Weakness 45

Day 7: Core Longing 51

Day 8: Directional Signals of the Enneagram 57

Day 9: Levels of Alignment with God's Truth 61

Day 10: When You Are Aligned 67
Day 11: When You Are Misaligned 71
Day 12: When You Are Out of Alignment Entirely 77
Day 13: The Wings 81
Day 14: The Triads 89
Day 15: Childhood Message 95
Day 16: Enneagram Paths 101
Day 17: Stress Path 107
Day 18: Blind Spot Path 113
Day 19: Growth Path 117
Day 20: Converging Path 123
Day 21: Moving Toward Your Best Self 129

Afterword 135
Acknowledgments 139
About the Author 143

Foreword

Learning about myself through the lens of the Enneagram has helped me tremendously. Before understanding myself as a Type 6, I always thought something was wrong with me. Being an anxious, overthinking, and worrisome person seemed to indicate I needed to change who I was (or so I thought). I feared these characteristics would not allow me to be successful. But as I studied more about the Enneagram, I learned that those negative beliefs weren't true. Though there are unhealthy levels of certain personality traits, I could figure out how to navigate and overcome them. With this greater self-awareness and self-assurance, my Type could be leveraged in a powerful way and used as a helpful tool to positively contribute to the world.

I discovered I could be more patient with myself and more compassionate toward others. Previously, my tendency was to view so many things as potentially dangerous—or I was overly suspicious of someone's behavior and hypervigilant of being taken advantage of me. But with the help of the Enneagram, I learned to recognize that I often feared what I didn't understand.

I've realized that while constantly overthinking and attempting to predict every scenario can be tiring, there are also advantages to this aspect of my personality. I'm grateful that as we come to understand ourselves better through the Enneagram, we can receive clearer guidance and the sense of direction we earnestly long for.

One of the joys I've come across on my Enneagram journey has been getting to know Beth; her husband, Jeff; and their kids. When I started following Beth's Instagram account, Your Enneagram Coach, she helped me navigate my 6-patterned mind-set. It was helpful to connect with Jeff, a fellow Type 6. Not only was it incredibly beneficial to have an experienced perspective on the traits of a Type 6, but it revealed a whole new approach to growing when I learned I could use this tool to exercise my faith in the Lord.

We don't have to be sure about everything to take steps forward in life. Otherwise, we wouldn't get to experience the power of acting in faith. There's beauty in letting go and learning to trust God more.

I hope you enjoy the transformative knowledge my friend Beth shares about the Type 6 in the pages ahead. May you learn to have more compassion for your thoughts and your own unique process of decision-making—and more faith in Christ as you learn to take healthy risks.

David Archuleta, Singer-Songwriter and Runner-Up, Season 7 of American Idol

Introduction

I'm so glad you're here! As an Enneagram teacher and coach, I have seen so many lives changed by the Enneagram. This is a perfect place for you to start your own journey of growth. I'll explain how this interactive book works, but first I'd like to share a little of my story.

Before I learned about the Enneagram, I often unknowingly committed *assumicide*, which is my word for damaging a relationship by assuming I know someone's thoughts, feelings, and motivations. I incorrectly guess why someone is behaving a particular way and respond (sometimes with disastrous results) without asking clarifying questions to confirm my assumptions or to find out what actually is going on. I've made many wrong and hurtful assumptions about people I dearly love, as well as destructive presumptions about myself.

When my husband, Jeff, and I were in the early years of our marriage, it was a difficult season in our relationship. For the life of me, I couldn't figure out Jeff, or myself. I had been a Christian since I was young and desired to live like Christ, but I kept running into the same stumbling blocks over and over again. I was constantly frustrated, and I longed to understand my heart's motives—*Why do I do what I do?* I figured understanding that might help jolt me out of my rut, but I didn't know where to start.

Then I learned about the insightful tool of the Enneagram, and it was exactly what I needed.

This personality typology (*ennea* for nine; *gram* for diagram) goes beyond what we do (our behaviors) and gets at *why* we do what we do (our heart's motives). And though there are just nine basic personality Types, each Type has multiple layers, allowing for numerous variations of any given personality Type.

The purpose of the Enneagram is to awaken self-awareness and provide hope for growth. Once we learn why each Type thinks, feels, and acts in specific ways, we can look at ourselves with new understanding. Then we can depend on God in new ways to reshape us. The Enneagram makes us aware of when our heart's motives are good and we are on the best path for our personality Type and when our heart is struggling and veering off course. The Enneagram is an insightful tool, but God's truth is what sets us free and brings transformation.

When I first learned about the Enneagram, I resonated with the Type 9—and had a good laugh when I discovered that 9s know themselves the least! But I finally had wisdom that cleared away the fog and illuminated my inner world. I kept thinking, *Oh, that's why I do that!* Everything started making sense, which brought my restless heart relief.

The Enneagram also helped me see when my

heart was aligned with God's truth, misaligned to some degree, or out of alignment entirely with the person God created me to be. It would highlight where I was misunderstanding myself or those I love, and then I could use that awareness to seek transformation. Using the Enneagram from this perspective was a significant turning point for me in all my relationships, especially my marriage. My new perspective allowed me to have more compassion, kindness, forgiveness, mercy, and grace toward others and myself.

Exploring my heart has been some of the hardest—and most rewarding—work I've ever done. The process of looking at our hearts exposes who we are at the core, which highlights our need for redemption and care from God, who is always supplying us with what we need. We simply need to come to Him and depend on Him to change us from the inside out. He will give us a new internal peace, joy, and security that will help us to flourish in new and life-giving ways. The Enneagram can function as an internal GPS, helping you understand why you and others think, feel, and behave in particular ways.

This internal GPS assists you in knowing your current location (your Main Enneagram Type) and your Type's healthiest destination (how your Type can live in alignment with the gospel).

The Enneagram also acts like a rumble strip on the highway—that boundary that makes an irritating sound when your car touches it, warning you when you're about to go off course. It keeps you from swerving into dangerous situations.

While everyone has character traits of all nine Types to varying degrees, we call only one our Main Type. In this book you will unlock some of the mysteries behind *why* you do what you do and discern ways you can grow into your best self.

If you're not sure of your Type number, that's okay! Going through the exercises will help you figure out what your Type number is. Sometimes it's helpful to find out what we're *not* as much as what we are. It's all about self-discovery and self-awareness.

If you find you resonate more with another number, that insight is valuable.

• • •

In the twenty-one entries that follow, we'll begin with a summary of your Type. Then we'll discuss topics that are general to the Enneagram and specific to your Type. Each reading will end with reflection questions—prompts to help you write out your thoughts, feelings, and gut reactions to what you have read. Putting pen to paper will help you focus and process what is going on inside you.

Before you begin, I want you to commit to observing your inner world from a nonjudgmental stance. Since God has fully forgiven us, we can observe ourselves without condemnation, guilt, or shame. Instead, we can rest in the fact that we are unconditionally loved, forgiven, and accepted based on what Christ did for us. Follow the prompts and write about your own story. Allow God to transform you from the inside out by helping you see yourself through the lens of the beautiful and amazing Type He designed you to be.

It's my privilege to walk with you as you discover who you are by examining your heart. I'm excited to be on this journey with you!

DEAR

TYPE 6

I'M THANKFUL FOR YOU BECAUSE...

You are trustworthy, loyal, reliable, deeply engaging, friendly, and playful. You treat everyone (including yourself) as an equal and work tirelessly to create stability and security in your world by bringing a cooperative spirit. And you are hardworking, persevering, and sacrificial for others.

OVERVIEW OF THE NINE ENNEAGRAM TYPES

The Enneagram (*ennea* = nine, *gram* = diagram) is a map for personal growth that identifies the nine basic ways of relating to and perceiving the world. It accurately describes *why* you think, feel, and behave in particular ways based upon your Core Motivations. Understanding the Enneagram will give you more self-awareness, forgiveness, and compassion for yourself and others.

To find your main Type, take our FREE assessment at test.YourEnneagramCoach.com, and find the Type on the next page that has your Core Motivations—what activates and drives your thoughts, feelings, and behaviors.

Core Motivations of Each Type

Core Desires: what you're always striving for, believing it will completely fulfill you

Core Fears: what you're always avoiding and trying to prevent from happening

Core Weakness: the issue you're always wrestling with, which will remain a struggle until you're in heaven and is a reminder you need God's help on a daily basis

Core Longing: the message your heart is always longing to hear

Type 1: MORAL PERFECTIONIST

Core Desire: Having integrity; being good, balanced, accurate, virtuous, and right.

Core Fear: Being wrong, bad, evil, inappropriate, unredeemable, or corruptible.

Core Weakness: *Resentment*: Repressing anger that leads to continual frustration and dissatisfaction with yourself, others, and the world for not being perfect.

Core Longing: You are good.

Type 2: SUPPORTIVE ADVISOR

Core Desire: Being appreciated, loved, and wanted.

Core Fear: Being rejected and unwanted; being thought worthless, needy, inconsequential, dispensable, or unworthy of love.

Core Weakness: *Pride*: Denying your own needs and emotions while using your strong intuition to discover and focus on the emotions and needs of others; confidently inserting your helpful support in hopes that others will say how grateful they are for your thoughtful care.

Core Longing: You are wanted and loved.

Type 3: SUCCESSFUL ACHIEVER

Core Desire: Having high status and respect; being admired, successful, and valuable.

Core Fear: Being exposed as or thought incompetent, inefficient, or worthless; failing to be or appear successful.

Core Weakness: *Deceit*: Deceiving yourself into believing that you are only the image you present to others; embellishing the truth by putting on a polished persona for everyone (including yourself) to see and admire.

Core Longing: You are loved for simply being you.

Type 4: ROMANTIC INDIVIDUALIST

Core Desire: Being unique, special, and authentic.

Core Fear: Being inadequate, emotionally cut off, plain, mundane, defective, flawed, or insignificant.

Core Weakness: *Envy*: Feeling that you're tragically flawed, that something foundational is missing inside you, and that others possess qualities you lack.

Core Longing: You are seen and loved for exactly who you are—special and unique.

Type 5: INVESTIGATIVE THINKER

Core Desire: Being capable and competent.

Core Fear: Being annihilated, invaded, or not existing; being thought incapable or ignorant; having obligations placed upon you, or your energy being completely depleted.

Core Weakness: *Avarice*: Feeling that you lack inner resources and that too much interaction with others will lead to catastrophic depletion; withholding yourself from contact with the world; holding on to your resources and minimizing your needs.

Core Longing: Your needs are not a problem.

Type 6: LOYAL GUARDIAN

Core Desire: Having security, guidance, and support.

Core Fear: Fearing fear itself; being without support, security, or guidance; being blamed, targeted, alone, or physically abandoned.

Core Weakness: *Anxiety*: Scanning the horizon of life and trying to predict and prevent negative outcomes (especially worst-case scenarios); remaining in a constant state of apprehension and worry.

Core Longing: You are safe and secure.

Type 7: ENTERTAINING OPTIMIST

Core Desire: Being happy, fully satisfied, and content.

Core Fear: Being deprived, trapped in emotional pain, limited, or bored; missing out on something fun.

Core Weakness: *Gluttony*: Feeling a great emptiness inside and having an insatiable desire to "fill yourself up" with experiences and stimulation in hopes of feeling completely satisfied and content.

Core Longing: You will be taken care of.

Type 8: PROTECTIVE CHALLENGER

Core Desire: Protecting yourself and those in your inner circle.

Core Fear: Being weak, powerless, harmed, controlled, vulnerable, manipulated, and left at the mercy of injustice.

Core Weakness: *Lust/Excess*: Constantly desiring intensity, control, and power; willfully pushing yourself on others in order to get what you desire.

Core Longing: You will not be betrayed.

Type 9: PEACEFUL MEDIATOR

Core Desire: Having inner stability and peace of mind.

Core Fear: Being in conflict, tension, or discord; feeling shut out and overlooked; losing connection and relationship with others.

Core Weakness: *Sloth*: Remaining in an unrealistic and idealistic world in order to keep the peace, remain easygoing, and not be disturbed by your anger; falling asleep to your passions, abilities, desires, needs, and worth by merging with others to keep peace and harmony.

Core Longing: Your presence matters.

TYPE 6

KEY MOTIVATIONS

Sixes want to have certainty, guidance, and feel supported. They want to feel safe and secure in relationships, so they will test their relationships to see how others react toward them. They want to remain loyal, committed, and defend their beliefs.

Overview of Type 6

The Loyal Guardian

Committed | Responsible
Faithful | Suspicious | Anxious

You are one of the most reliable, hardworking, and dutiful people out there. Your steadiness, sense of humor, and ability to foresee problems make you an incredible team player. Genuinely concerned about the common good, you can hold groups together.

However, below the surface, you regularly struggle with fear and uncertainty, viewing the world as a dangerous place. You are prone to see and assume the worst, so you are hypervigilant, always scanning for possible threats. You manage your anxiety by preemptively running through worst-case scenarios. You're constantly thinking, *But what about this? What about that?*

When you forget God's love for you, you can suffer from self-doubt, worry, and catastrophic thinking, which leaves you unable to relax. Your mind can become muddled, skeptical, and hesitant to make decisions. You will focus on planning for crises to give you a sense of control and safety, aiming to create a life that is trouble-free and predictable.

In relationships, you can struggle with projecting your fears, doubts, and insecurities onto others as a means to protect yourself. These misplaced suspicions often erode your trust in others, God, and yourself.

However, when your heart aligns with God's truth, and you learn to take your fears and anxiety to Him, you experience a transformation that brings forth great courage in your life. You realize you are secure in Him, begin to trust yourself, and experience a peace that surpasses your fears. As you are unhindered by your weaknesses and your strengths shine, the world is blessed by your dedication, wit, ability to solve problems, and genuine loyalty.

DAY 1

Faith and the Enneagram

Is your heart a mystery to you? Do you need help using the knowledge the Enneagram offers to improve your life? If that's where you are, I'm happy to tell you that there is help, and there is hope.

The Bible teaches that God cares about our heart's motives. He "sees not as man sees: man looks on the outward appearance, but the LORD looks on the heart" (1 Samuel 16:7). So we shouldn't look only at our external behaviors; we also need to examine our inner world. For most of us, it's no surprise that the heart of our problem is the problem of our heart!

Before we begin discussing the Enneagram in depth, I'd like to share my beliefs with you for two reasons: First, it's a critical part of how I'll guide you through the Enneagram principles. Second, my faith is what sustains and encourages me, and I believe the same will be true for you.

I believe the Bible is God's truth and the ultimate authority for our lives. Through it, we learn about God's character, love, and wisdom. It brings us close to Him and guides us in the best way to live. My relationship with God brought me healing and purpose before I ever heard of the Enneagram.

Jesus has not been optional for my personal growth; He has been absolutely and utterly vital. He has always come alongside me with love, compassion, and mercy.

I've always wanted my faith to be the most important part of my life, but I spent years frustrated, running into the same issues in my heart over and over again. The Enneagram helped me understand my heart's motives.

As you think about your Type, I'll help you look

at your heart, your life, and your relationships through the lens of the Enneagram. I'll also teach you ways to understand yourself and others and to develop patience and empathy for your differences.

With God working in you and helpful insights from the Enneagram to change awareness and actions, you'll grow into the person you'd like to be more than you've ever dared to dream possible.

When you place your faith in Jesus Christ as your Savior, three life-changing questions are answered, bringing you ultimate grace and freedom:

Am I fully accepted by God (even with all the mess and sin in my life)?

Yes! You are declared righteous. Christ not only purchased forgiveness for your sin but also gave you His perfect righteousness.

Am I loved by God?

Yes! God cherishes you and wants you to be close to Him. He adopted you, making you His beloved child.

Is it really possible for me to change?

Yes! You are being made new. This both *happened* to you and *is happening* to you. This means that you are changed because of what Christ has done, and you are continuing to change as you grow in Christ (it's a bit of a paradox). You can live in an ongoing process of growth by working with the Holy Spirit to become more like Christ, who loves you and gave Himself up for you.

These three life-changing events are what we mean by God's truth, the good news of Christ's finished work on our behalf—"the gospel."

Receiving God's truth and learning about the Enneagram will give you a deeper and richer understanding of *who you are* and *Whose you are*.

When we know *who we are*, we understand our heart's motives and needs and can see God reaching out to meet our needs and giving us grace for our sins through Christ.

And when we know *Whose we are*, we understand that because of Christ's sacrifice on our behalf, we're God's cherished children. He comforts, sustains, and delights in us. Because of God's character, His love never changes; it doesn't depend on us "getting better" or "doing better" since it hinges solely on what Christ has already done for us. He loves us and desires for us to be in a relationship with Him. We become more like Him by surrendering to Him and depending on the Holy Spirit to transform us.

Which leads us back to looking at who we are. Bringing our faith and the Enneagram together helps us hear God's truths in our mother tongue (kind of like our personality Type's unique language), which enables us to understand God's truth more deeply and will lead to transformation.

Going Deeper

What things have you longed to change about yourself?

How have you attempted to rescue yourself in the past or bring about change on your own? How successful were you?

What difference does knowing you belong to God make in your life?

Being Aware

We can't do anything to make God love us more or love us less since our relationship status has been taken care of solely through Christ's finished work on our behalf. And yet that doesn't mean we're not responsible for participating in our growth. That growth path will look different for different personality Types. We can use the Enneagram to help us find our unique path for transformation as we continue learning and growing. And that's what's super fun about the Enneagram! This insightful tool helps us discover *who we are* and *Whose we are*.

We are not alone in this journey of growth. God is with us, sustaining us and providing for us. Although we're all uniquely made and no one is alike (it boggles the mind to think about it!), there are commonalities in how we think, feel, and act. The Enneagram shows us nine basic personality Types, each with its own specific patterns of thinking and ways of being: nine *valid* perspectives of the world. Getting to know each of these personality Types increases understanding, compassion, mercy, grace, and forgiveness toward ourselves and others.

Our creative God made us so diverse, yet we all reflect the essence of His character: wise, caring, radiant, creative, protective, insightful, joyful, knowledgeable, and peaceful. As we learn about ourselves and others from the Enneagram, we also learn more about God. Our strengths reflect His attributes.

So how do we begin to find our unique path for growth? By learning about the Enneagram, and by becoming aware of how our heart is doing, which isn't always easy for us. It takes a great deal of time and intentional focus. We start by observing our inner world from a *nonjudgmental* stance. (I don't know how to emphasize this enough!)

Then we can begin to recognize patterns, pause while we are in the present circumstance, and ask ourselves good, clarifying questions about *why* we are thinking, feeling, or behaving in particular ways. We can begin to identify those frustrating patterns we repeat over and over again (the ones we haven't been able to figure out how to stop) and start to think about why we keep doing them.

As I've said before, the Enneagram can act like a rumble strip on a highway, warning you when you're heading off your best path. It lets you know that if you continue in the same direction, drowsy or distracted, you might hurt yourself and others. Alerts about impending danger allow you to course correct, avoid heartache, and experience greater freedom. You will create new patterns of behavior, including a new way of turning to God, when you start to notice the rumble strips in your life.

When you're sensing a rumble strip warning, focus on the acronym AWARE:

- *Awaken*: Notice how you are reacting in your behavior, feelings, thoughts, and body sensations.
- *Welcome*: Be open to what you might learn and observe without condemnation and shame.
- *Ask*: Ask God to help clarify what is happening internally.
- *Receive*: Receive any insight and affirm your true identity as God's beloved child.
- *Enjoy*: Enjoy your new freedom from old self-defeating patterns of living.

Going Deeper

As you look back on your life, when would you have liked a rumble strip to warn you of danger?

In general, what causes you to veer off course and land in a common pitfall (for example, when you're worried)?

SHARING WITH OTHERS HOW BEST TO LOVE ME

Speak to me in a clear
and direct manner.

Carefully listen to all my thoughts
as I verbally process.

Encourage me by reassuring
me that things will be okay.

Have a good sense of humor,
and enjoy laughing and
joking around with me.

Tell me and show me you are
supportive and committed to me.

Acknowledge that I am loyal,
dutiful, and responsible.

Core Motivations

We'll begin discussing the fundamentals of the Enneagram by looking at our motivations. Your Core Motivations are the driving force behind your thoughts, feelings, and actions. The internal motivations specific to your Type help explain why you do what you do.

(This is why it's impossible to discern someone else's Type. We don't know what motivates them to think, feel, and behave in particular ways. It's their Core Motivations, not their actions, that determine their Type.)

These Core Motivations consist of:

- *Core Fear*: what you're always avoiding and trying to prevent from happening
- *Core Desire*: what you're always striving for, believing it will completely fulfill you
- *Core Weakness*: the issue you're always wrestling with, which will remain a struggle until you're in heaven and is a reminder you need God's help on a daily basis
- *Core Longing*: the message your heart longs to hear

The Enneagram, like a nonjudgmental friend, names and addresses these dynamics of your heart. When you use the Enneagram from a faith-centered approach, you can see how Christ's finished work on your behalf has already satisfied your Core Longing and resolved your Core Fear, Core Desire, and Core Weakness. It's a process to learn how to live in that reality.

When we stray from the truth that we are God's beloved children, it's harder to look inside. After all,

Scripture tells us that "the heart is deceitful . . . and desperately sick" (Jeremiah 17:9). When we forget God's unconditional love for us, we respond to our weaknesses and vulnerabilities with shame or contempt, leaving us feeling worse.

When we only focus on obeying externally, we attempt to look good on the outside but never deal with the source of all our struggles on the inside.

However, when we allow ourselves to rest in the truth that Christ took care of everything for us, we can look at our inner world without fear or condemnation. Real transformation begins when we own our shortcomings.

Here are the Core Motivations of a Type 6:

- *Core Fear*: feeling fear itself; being without security, guidance, or support; being blamed, targeted, alone, or physically abandoned
- *Core Desire*: having security, guidance, and support
- *Core Weakness*: having anxiety;

scanning the horizon of life and trying to predict and prevent negative outcomes (especially worst-case scenarios); remaining in a constant state of apprehension and worry

- *Core Longing*: "You are safe and secure."

The Enneagram exposes the condition of our hearts, and it will tear down any facade we try to hide behind. Since we are God's saved children, we don't have to be afraid of judgment. We can be vulnerable because we know God has taken care of us perfectly through Christ—He has forgiven us and set us free from fear, condemnation, and shame. His presence is a safe place where we can be completely honest about where we are. With this freedom, allow the Enneagram to be a flashlight to your heart's condition. Let it reveal how you are doing at any given moment so you can remain on the best path for your personality Type.

Going Deeper

How challenging is it for you to look at the condition of your heart?

What response do you typically have when you recognize your struggles?

How would you like to respond when the struggles inside you are exposed?

DAY 4

Core Fear

Understanding your Core Fear is the first step in identifying your motivations. Your personality believes it's vital to your well-being that you constantly spend time and energy avoiding this thing you fear. It is the lens through which you see the world, the "reality" you believe. You assume others do, or should, see the world through this lens, and you may become confused and dismayed when they don't.

Your Core Fear as a Type 6 is feeling fear itself; being without security, guidance, or support; and being blamed, targeted, alone, or physically abandoned.

You don't want to feel unsafe or uncertain. You don't want to be pressured to do something that will get you in trouble, to be forced to accept new ideas quickly, or to have your beliefs questioned by an outsider.

Even though you're afraid of feeling fear itself and feeling alone, here's what is true: God is with you, and His presence can overpower your fear. He created the universe. He is all-powerful, all-knowing, all-providing, and all-sustaining. He can do anything and handle anything!

God is also good, and you can trust Him with your anxieties and worries. He is not shocked by them. In fact, He came to free you from them. He wants you to rest your weary and worried heart on Him and allow Him to protect you and provide for you.

When your Core Fears get activated, use them as a rumble strip to alert you. Then pause, become AWARE, and reorient yourself with what is true so your heart can rest in His security.

MY CORE FEARS

TYPE 6 THE LOYAL GUARDIAN

Feeling fear itself; being without support, security, or guidance; being blamed, targeted, alone, or physically abandoned

Going Deeper

What comes to mind when you think about your Core Fear?

Do any particular words in the Type 6 Core Fear description ring true for you?

What strategies have you used in the past to protect yourself from your fears?

DAY 5

Core Desire

Understanding your Core Desire is the next step in identifying your motivations. Your Core Desire is what you're always striving for, believing it will ultimately fulfill you.

While your personality Type is running away from your Core Fear, it's also running toward your Core Desire. You believe that once you have this Core Desire met, all of life will be okay and you will feel fully satisfied and content. This longing to experience your Core Desire constantly propels you to focus your efforts on pursuing and obtaining it.

As a Type 6, you desire security, guidance, and support. You want a sense of certainty so you can make good decisions, and you look for trustworthy people or belief systems to provide wisdom and direction.

God knows your Core Desire, and He freely gives it to you. You are 100 percent secure in being God's dearly loved child. He delights in you and desires to be close to you!

He already protects you and provides for you daily. He knows your struggles and wants to bring more assurance and peace to your heart. His Word gives you guidance in life.

Not everyone has the same Core Desire as you. Take time to recognize that others are just as passionate in obtaining their Core Desire as you are in getting yours. This awareness will help you navigate relationship dynamics, enabling you to offer more empathy, compassion, and grace. Use the Enneagram to know yourself better so you can better communicate with others about what is happening inside your heart. Then be curious about others, and ask them to reveal to you their desires so you can get to know them on a deeper level.

MY CORE DESIRES

TYPE 6 THE LOYAL GUARDIAN

Having security, guidance, and support

Going Deeper

As you look back over your life, what aspects of the Type 6 Core Desire have you been chasing?

Describe ways you have attempted to pursue these specific desires.

What would it feel like to trust in the fact that God has already met your Core Desire?

Core Weakness

Deep inside, you struggle with a Core Weakness, which is your Achilles' heel. This one issue repeatedly causes you to stumble in life. At times you might find some relief. But as hard as you try to improve on your own, your struggle in this area continually resurfaces.

God's encouraging words to you are that when you are weak, He is strong. This brings hope that you are not destined to be utterly stuck in your weakness. As you grow closer to God and depend on Him, He will lessen the constraint your Core Weakness has over you and help you move out of your rut.

As a Type 6, your Core Weakness is *anxiety*. You scan the horizon of life to predict and prevent negative outcomes (especially worst-case scenarios) and remain in a constant state of apprehension and worry. Every Type 6 has an inner committee constantly shouting feedback and cautions at them, like the Parliament in England. The internal clamor causes so much confusion, anxiety, and self-doubt that you do not know what to decide. To feel safe and secure, you go outside yourself to find support and guidance from a trusted person or belief system.

God, who created all things, never makes a mistake. He delights in sustaining you, His creation, and providing you with what you need. He knows you intimately and cares for you.

By focusing on the fact that you already have security, you can cease striving to control future outcomes and trust in Him. He is God, and you are not. What a relief! Bring Him all your burdens and worries, and He will guide you in living lightly and freely.

When you see your Core Weakness surfacing, think of it as a rumble strip alerting you that you can easily veer off course into your common pitfalls of worst-case thinking, suspiciousness, and worry. Use this awareness to "recalculate" your inner world so you can get back to your healthiest path.

Going Deeper

What comes to mind as you think about your Core Weakness?

In what ways have you wrestled with anxiety throughout your life?

What specific things are you facing now that your Core Weakness impacts?

MY CORE WEAKNESS

TYPE 6 THE LOYAL GUARDIAN

Anxiety — scanning the horizon of life and trying to predict and prevent negative outcomes (especially worst-case scenarios); remaining in a constant state of apprehension and worry

Core Longing

Your Core Longing is the message your heart is always yearning to receive, what you've craved since you were a child. Throughout life, you've been striving to hear this message from your family members, friends, teachers, coaches, and bosses. No matter how much you've tried to get others to communicate this message to you, you've never felt it was delivered to the degree your heart needed it.

As a Type 6, your Core Longing is to hear, "You are safe and secure."

You have believed that if you could be prepared and cautious enough to prevent bad things from happening, then others would communicate this message to you, whether in verbal or nonverbal ways. However, even those who have tried their best to do this for you are unable to satisfy this longing that runs so deep inside you.

Why? Because people *cannot* give you all you need. Only God can. When you're trying to receive this message apart from God, you will always thirst for more. But when you listen to Him and see that He's drawing you to Himself, then you will find fulfillment and freedom.

How does God meet your Core Longing?

1. **He is all-powerful, and you are safe in His care.**

   You feel that you are all alone and need to protect yourself from uncertainty and danger. Being a human, you cannot accomplish this. But God can and He will because He loves you and protects you with His wisdom and strength.

2. **The Holy Spirit gives you clarity and certainty in a confusing and chaotic world.**

> Your inner committee gives too many contradictory messages, causing paralyzing confusion and doubt. The Holy Spirit, however, provides you clarity, peace, and assurance. He will let you know that you are not alone, and He will guide you in every way.

When you feel uncertain and insecure, use the Enneagram as the rumble strip to alert you of what is true: that you are safe and secure in God. Allow it to point out how you are believing false messages so you can live a more secure and freeing life.

Going Deeper

How have you seen your Core Longing at work in your life?

_____

_____

_____

_____

What did that look like when you were a child?

How does it appear in your life as an adult?

Describe how you feel and what you think when you read that God answers your longing.

MY CORE LONGING

TYPE 6 THE LOYAL GUARDIAN

The message my heart always longs to hear.

"You are safe."

Directional Signals of the Enneagram

Just as a GPS gives directional signals such as "Approaching right turn" or "Proceed to the highlighted route," the Enneagram guides us in which way to go. But we still need to pay attention to where we're heading and reroute our course when necessary.

The Enneagram provides directions in a couple of ways: (1) by pointing out how aligned with God's truth we are, and (2) by showing us what other Types we are connected to and how we might take on those Types' characteristics in different life situations. We do not *become* the Types we are

HOW TO USE YOUR ENNEAGRAM

YOUR INTERNAL GPS

It reveals ***why*** you think, feel, and behave in particular ways, so you can steer your internal life in the best direction for your personality type.

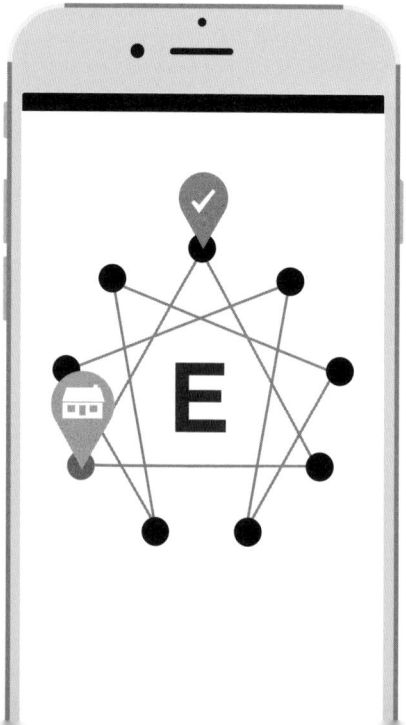

connected to; we remain our Main Type (with its Core Fear, Desire, Weakness, and Longing) as we access the other Types' attributes.

The directional signals of the Enneagram make us aware of which way our heart is heading and where we might end up. Whether it's a good or bad direction depends on various factors—it can change day by day as we take on positive or negative qualities of other Types.

When headed in the wrong direction, the steps to turning around and getting back on track are simply owning our mistakes, turning from them, asking for forgiveness from God and others, and asking God to restore us to the best path.

The directional signals we'll discuss in the following entries are: the Levels of Alignment with God's Truth, the Wings, the Triads, and the Enneagram Paths. Hang in there! I'll guide you through these signals, which will help you discover who you are and Whose you are, and show you the healthiest path for your personality Type.

Levels of Alignment with God's Truth

The first set of directional signals we'll discuss are the Levels of Alignment with God's truth. The inspiration for these levels comes from the apostle Paul, who wrote in Galatians 2:14 that some of the early Christian leaders' conduct was not in step (aligned) with God's truth. To grow in our particular personality Type, we must be in step with God's truth and design for us.

We all move fluidly through the Levels of Alignment from day to day. The level at which we find ourselves at any given moment depends on our heart's condition and how we're navigating through life.

Healthy	Aligned with God's Truth (Living as His Beloved)
Average (Autopilot)	Misaligned with God's Truth (Living in Our Own Strength)
Unhealthy	Out of Alignment with God's Truth (Living as an Orphan)

When we are resting, believing, and trusting in who we are in Christ, we are living as His beloved (healthy and aligned with God's truth). We are no longer using our personality strategies to meet our needs and desires. Instead, we are coming to our God, who we know loves us and will provide for us.

When our heart and mind begin to wander from that truth, we start to believe that we must take some control and live in our own strength, even though He is good and sovereign (average/autopilot level).

Then there are times when we completely forget that we are His beloved children. In this state of mind, we think we're all alone, that we're orphans who have to handle all of life on our own (unhealthy level).

But no matter where we are on the Levels of Alignment, we are always His cherished children. Christ's life, death, and resurrection accomplished everything required for us to be His. Therefore, no matter what state our heart is in, we can *rejoice* in His work in our lives, *repent* if we need to, and fully *rest* in who we are in Him.

As you can imagine, a group of people with the same personality Type (same Core Fear, Desire, Weakness, and Longing) can look vastly different from each other due to varying alignments with God's truth.

In the readings that follow, we will consider how you as a Type 6 function at the three Levels of Alignment.

Going Deeper

At what Level of Alignment do you think your heart is at the moment?

In what season of life have you thrived the most, not feeling limited by your fears and weaknesses?

What do you think contributed to that growth?

DAY 10

When You Are Aligned

When the condition of your heart is healthy, you align with God's truth that you are fully taken care of by Christ.

As a Type 6 at this level, you take your anxieties and insecurities to God, acknowledging that He can care for you. Because you know that God is good to His children, you trust Him instead of trying to predict and control life on your own. You understand that safety and security are never certain on earth, but God will always be there to love you, protect you, and provide for you. You trust that He is always close by, caring for your every need.

Relying on His guidance enables you to lead

from a place of true courage, positive thinking, thoughtful leadership, and rich self-expression.

Trust is essential to you. Therefore, you will form bonds, build long-term relationships, and make alliances with others. These ties bring you a sense of security.

You are warm, loving, witty, playful, and a great troubleshooter. Thoughtful of others, you enjoy collaborating with a group. Others can rely on you to fulfill your commitments.

Going Deeper

When are you at your best and most trusting of God?

What differences do you notice in your thinking and in your life when you're in that state?

What helps you stay in alignment with God's plan for your personality Type?

Write about a time when you exhibited true courage, strong leadership, or any other indicators of healthy alignment.

DAY 11

When You Are Misaligned

Even though we know God is good and in control, there are times when our hearts and minds wander away from the truth that God loves us and has fully provided for us in the finished work of Christ on our behalf. In this average or autopilot level of health, we start to believe that we must take some control and live in our own strength.

As a Type 6 at this level, you invest time and energy into whatever you believe will bring you safety and certainty. You look to your alliances and authorities for security and assurance. Always anticipating problems, you become vigilant about protecting yourself from harm.

To resist having more demands placed on you, you become avoidant, cautious, uncertain, and passive-aggressive or highly reactive, anxious, and pessimistic, while giving others mixed signals. Your internal confusion makes you procrastinate, be indecisive, and behave unpredictably.

To compensate for your insecurities, you become sarcastic, defensive, and belligerent, blaming others for your problems and taking a tough stance toward outsiders. You divide people into friends and enemies while looking for threats to your security. You can be authoritarian while also being fearful of authority, suspicious, and conspiratorial.

MY HIDDEN STRUGGLE

TYPE 6

The constant need for inner calm and to make the world feel trouble-free and predictable

Anxiety from an "internal committee" of voices constantly chiming in worst-case scenarios, contradictory thoughts, and questions, making me second-guess myself and what I know

The inability to think clearly and make sound decisions when my mind is always in a hypervigilant state

Going Deeper

What aspects of your behavior and life indicate that you are becoming misaligned?

In what ways do you attempt to live in your own strength, not in your identity as a person God loves?

What can you do when you begin to catch yourself in misalignment?

When You Are Out of Alignment Entirely

When we forget that our status never changes, and we are still His beloved based on what Christ did for us, we think and believe we're all alone, like an orphan.

Your whole world at this level revolves around identifying danger. Forgetting that God cares immensely for you, you think you've been abandoned in this world. You become hypervigilant and suspicious of everyone. Leaning toward paranoia, you project your insecurities and feelings onto others, which causes more distrust and harm in your relationships.

Because 6s don't trust their thinking and decision-making ability, you seek a trustworthy authority to follow. However, you have difficulty trusting anyone, so you sabotage relationships by testing these authority figures. This ultimately makes you more cynical and isolated and produces more anxiety and fear.

This cycle will continue until you realize that God is a loving and caring Father to you. When you begin to believe this truth and depend on Him completely, you will move up the levels of health.

Going Deeper

In what seasons of life have you been most out of alignment with God's truth?

What does this level look like for you (specific behaviors, beliefs, etc.)?

Who in your life can best support and encourage you when you're struggling and guide you back to health?

The Wings

The next set of directional signals we'll discuss are the Wings, which are the two numbers *directly* next to your Main Type's number on the Enneagram diagram. As I've said, we access the characteristics of the Type on either side of us while remaining our Main Type. So everyone's Enneagram personality is a combination of one Main Type and the two Types adjacent to it.

As a Type 6, your Wings are 5 and 7. You'll often see it written this way: 6w5 or 6w7.

Everyone uses their Wings to varying degrees and differently in different circumstances, but it's common for a person to rely more on one Wing than another.

You can think of the Wings like salt and pepper. Each Wing adds a unique "flavor" to your personality, bringing complexity to your Main Type. Just as a delicious filet mignon doesn't *become* the salt or pepper we season it with, we don't become our Wings. Our Wings influence our Main Type in varying ways, both positively and negatively depending on where we are on the Levels of Alignment. We know that too much salt or pepper can make that filet inedible, but the right balance can enhance our enjoyment of it significantly.

When we align with God's truth, we can access the healthy aspects of our Wings. When we are misaligned or out of alignment with God's truth, we will often draw from the average or unhealthy aspects of our Wings. And like under seasoning or over seasoning our perfectly cooked steaks, it can make a huge difference.

Learning how to use our Wings correctly can dramatically alter our life experiences. Applying "seasoning"—utilizing the healthy attributes of our Wings—can help us change course. As we return to believing and trusting in God, we can express ourselves more fully and be seen for who we really are.

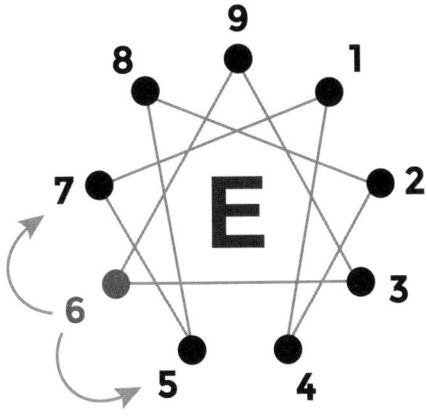

Type 6 with Wing 5 (6w5), The Defender: Types 6 and 5 conflict with each other. Type 6 wants to unite with others for security and support, while Type 5 seeks to detach from others and get security from knowledge.

If you're a Defender, you protect the underdog and gravitate toward a system of beliefs to provide guidance and security. Self-controlled, responsible, and serious about your ethical and political views, you can be mistyped as a 1. You can also be outspoken and intense, looking like an 8.

You are organized, perceptive, and involved with people you consider to be competent and knowledgeable. You may have a mentor or two for guidance. Defenders are often suspicious, cerebral, and watchful for potential adversaries.

Type 6 with Wing 7 (6w7), The Buddy: Types 6 and 7 easily blend together. If you're a Buddy, you are extroverted, supportive, witty, friendly, and likable. You read the reactions of others to assess where you stand with them. Many friends and mentors provide you with security, support, and guidance.

You seek enjoyment in life even with anxiety in the background. When you are struggling, you can be tense and hardworking, yet procrastinate out of fear. Buddies can be more reactive than Defenders when experiencing pressure to make a decision quickly.

Type 6 WINGS

Type 6 with a 5 Wing (6w5)
"The Defender"
They are more introverted, intellectual, cautious, focused, paranoid, anxious, and standoffish.

Type 6 with 7 Wing (6w7)
"The Buddy"
They are more extroverted, materialistic, sociable, playful, funny, energetic, active, and impulsive.

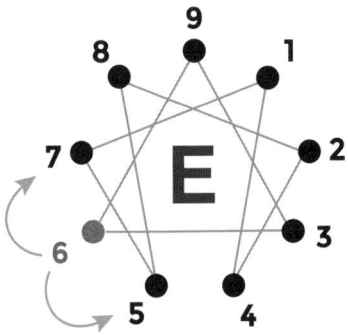

Going Deeper

Which Wing do you use more?

How have you seen this Wing enhance your Main Type?

How does it impact your relationships, work, and everyday life?

How does the other Wing influence your Main Type?

How can you utilize it more to create balance?

The Triads

The next set of directional signals we'll discuss are the Triads. We can group the nine personality Types in many ways, and the most common one is by groupings of three, or Triads. The three Types in each group share common assets and liabilities. For each person one Triad is more dominant (the one with your Main Type) than the other two.

Though we could name several different Triads within the Enneagram, the best known is the Center of Intelligence Triad:

- Feeling Center (Heart Triad): Types 2, 3, and 4
- Thinking Center (Head Triad): Types 5, 6, and 7
- Instinctive Center (Gut Triad): Types 8, 9, and 1

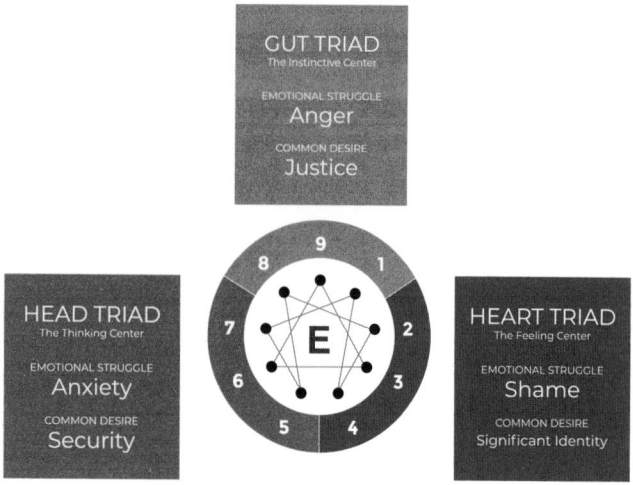

Two commonalities drive the Enneagram Types in each of these three centers: a common emotional imbalance and a common desire.

In the Head Triad, Types 5, 6, and 7 are imbalanced in their *thinking*. They all have similar assets and liabilities related to how they think and engage in life through mental analysis. They all react to their *mental struggles* with *anxiety* (or fear). Type 5s are anxious about not knowing enough to go out into the world and do. Type 6s are anxious about all the negative possibilities that could happen in any given situation. Type 7s are anxious about being forced to focus on their inner world, getting trapped in emotional pain, or feeling deprived.

Those in the Head Triad focus on a desire for *security*. Type 5s seek security through knowledge and understanding. Type 6s seek security in identifying all possible scenarios, planning for the future, and having a support system in place. Type 7s seek security by avoiding their inner world of anxiety and experiencing fun, stimulation, and excitement from the external world.

When you are healthy as a Type 6, you think systematically and can predict potential problems. A very loyal and committed friend, you look for similar qualities in others.

However, when you begin to struggle, you doubt your ability to make good decisions, so you look outside yourself for discernment and gain "permission" from an authority figure or belief system to make choices. This dependence allows you to feel guided and supported.

ENNEAGRAM TYPE 6

At Their Best	At Their Worst
Loyal	Hypervigilant
Likable	Dependent
Prepared	Unpredictable
Trustworthy	Judgmental
Compassionate	Paranoid
Witty	Defensive
Practical	Rigid
Supportive	Self-Defeating
Responsible	Self-Doubting

You find others on your side to help you feel secure and protected. Sadly, when you are struggling, you can become suspicious, fearful, and doubting, even toward your allies. This attitude can provoke others to leave you, causing the abandonment and insecurity you so desperately try to avoid.

Going Deeper

What stands out to you about being in the Head Triad and your tendency to get stuck in your thoughts?

How attuned are you to your feelings and gut instincts in comparison to thinking?

In what ways do you wrestle with anxiety and look outside yourself for direction? Does it bring the security you desire?

Where do your strengths of loyalty, commitment, and preparedness shine the most?

Childhood Message

Before we discuss the last set of directional signals (the Enneagram Paths), we need to understand what the Enneagram calls a Childhood Message.

From birth, everyone has a unique perspective on life, our personality Type's perspective. We all tend toward particular assumptions or concerns, and these develop into a Childhood Message. Our parents, teachers, and authority figures may have directly communicated this message to us, but most of the time, we interpreted what they said or did through the lens of our personality Type to fit this belief.

Sometimes we can see a direct correlation between our Childhood Message and a childhood event; other times we can't. Somewhere, somehow, we picked up a message that rang true for us because of our personality Type's hardwiring. This false interpretation of our circumstances was and still is painful to us, profoundly impacting us as children and as adults.

Gaining insight into how our personality Type interpreted events and relationships in childhood will help us identify how that interpretation is impacting us today. Believing our Childhood Message causes our personality to reinforce its strategies to protect us from our Core Fear—apart from God's truth. Once we understand the message is hardwired into our thinking, we can experience God's healing truth and live more freely.

What's more, when we know the Childhood Message of others, we can begin to understand why they do what they do and how we can communicate with them more effectively.

As a Type 6, your Childhood Message is: "It is not okay to trust yourself."

The message your heart longed to hear as a child is your Core Longing: "You are safe and secure."

• • •

Type 6s grew up feeling that the world was dangerous and unreliable, which caused them to gravitate toward a protective figure in their lives. They desired the guidance and support that should come from a caregiver, but since they never believed they received it fully, they took on the role of caregiver themselves.

To avoid chaos, harm, or insecurity, they learned to predict what could go wrong, strategize a way to dodge it or handle it, and develop alliances with others. Finding a support system is very important for Type 6s to feel safe.

Early in life Type 6s developed an "inner committee," a series of internal voices pointing out potential dangers. Each voice would be associated with different viewpoints and concerns. All would push Type 6 children to prepare for every possible scenario to ensure harm could not invade their world.

This inner committee created a lot of confusion for Type 6 children since the viewpoints came from different angles. They couldn't discern which one to follow, so they sought outside guidance from authority figures. But since their minds were always coming up with worst-case scenarios, they tended to become suspicious of their authority figures as well. Therefore, their inner committee created more anxiety than it helped, causing self-doubt and confusion.

Type 6s carry the anxiety, caution, and insecurity from their childhood into adulthood. They need to trust that God has given them great discernment skills and insights to navigate life and make their own decisions.

You can trust that God will direct you, so listen to His clear, reassuring, and peaceful direction, and follow that instead of the chaotic and confusing inner committee.

Knowing your personality Type's Childhood Message will help you break free from childhood perceptions and reinterpret pieces of your story from a better vantage point. As you explore this, be gracious to yourself and your past. Be sensitive, nonjudgmental, caring, and kind to yourself. And remember, only God can fully redeem your past. He can free you from chains that bind, heal wounds that linger, and restore you to freedom.

Going Deeper

To what degree do you relate to the Type 6 Childhood Message?

What stories come to mind when you hear it?

What circumstances in the present have repeated this message from the past?

What advice would you give to your childhood self in light of this message?

DAY 16

Enneagram Paths

The final directional signals we'll discuss are the Enneagram Paths, which the inner lines and arrows in the Enneagram diagram display. The lines and arrows going out from our Main Type point to our Connecting Types. As a Type 6, you connect to Types 3 and 9.

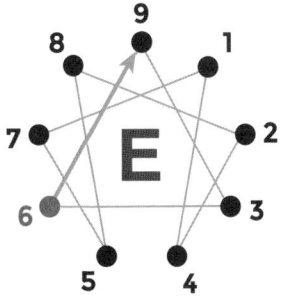

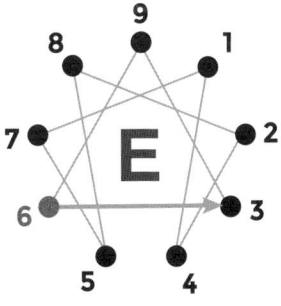

Remember, we can access both positive and negative characteristics of a Type we are connected to. The kind we access depends on whether we are aligned, misaligned, or out of alignment with God's truth.

Here is an overview of the four Enneagram Paths, which we'll discuss further in the following readings:

- *Stress Path*: When we're under stress, we tend to take on some of the misaligned or out-of-alignment characteristics of our Stress Path Type. For Type 6, these are the negative aspects of Type 3.
- *Blind Spot Path*: When we're around those we're most familiar with (mainly family), we display the misaligned characteristics of our Blind Spot Path Type. We typically do not see these characteristics in ourselves easily. For Type 6, these are the negative aspects of Type 9.
- *Growth Path*: When we believe and trust

that God loves us and that all He has is ours in Christ, we begin to move in a healthier direction, accessing the aligned characteristics of our Connecting Type. For Type 6, these are the positive aspects of Type 9.

- *Converging Path*: After making progress on the Growth path, we can reach the most aligned point of our Type, which is where three healthy Types come together. Here we access the healthiest qualities of our Main Type, our Growth Path's Type, and our Stress Path's Type.

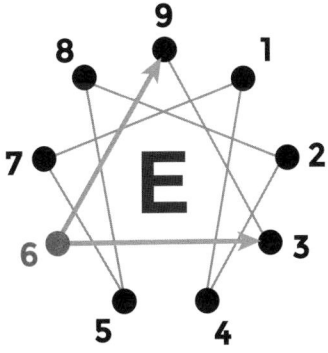

Going Deeper

In what direction is your heart currently heading?

What concerns are you wrestling with?

What growth have you experienced recently?

When you look at the four paths, what path have you been traveling recently? Why?

DAY 17

Stress Path

Under stress, you tend to move in the direction of the arrow below, taking on some of the misaligned characteristics of Type 3. Learning to identify these behavior patterns can serve as a rumble strip warning that you're veering off course. Then you can

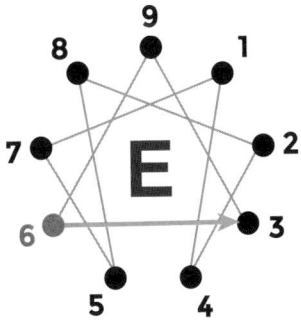

stop, pray for God's help, and move in a healthier direction for your personality.

As a Type 6 moving toward the average or unhealthy Type 3, you may:

- arrogantly believe that you alone can see all possible scenarios.
- keep yourself busy to avoid feeling anxious.
- refuse to try something new if you might fail.
- worry about your self-image and what others might be thinking of you.
- design your behavior to gain security and alliances with others.
- use charm and a likable persona to establish support and loyalties with others.

Going Deeper

Describe a stressful time when you took on some of these tendencies.

What was the situation, and why were you triggered to respond this way?

When have you become overwhelmed and avoided feeling anxious by keeping busy?

What things in your life cause the most stress for you?

TYPE 6 UNDER STRESS

When under stress, **Type 6** will start to exhibit some of the average to unhealthy characteristics of **Type 3**.

Become competitive and arrogant

Avoid feeling anxiety by being busy

Reluctant to try anything new if failure is a possibility

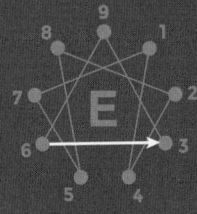

Blind Spot Path

When you're around people you're most familiar with—family members or close friends—you express yourself more freely. You show them parts of yourself you don't show anyone else, for better or worse. When you're uninhibited and not at your best, you display the negative qualities of your personality. On this Blind Spot Path, you access the misaligned attributes of your Connecting Type, which is Type 9.

You may be unaware that you're behaving differently with your family members or close friends than you are with other people. Be sure to take note of this path when you're trying to understand yourself and your reactions, because it may surprise you. Working on these negative aspects can improve the relationship dynamics with those you're closest to.

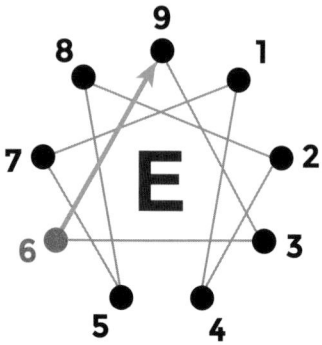

As a Type 6 moving toward the average or unhealthy Type 9, you may:

- deal with stress by shutting down.
- react negatively to interruptions or disturbances.
- stubbornly resist others' demands when you're overwhelmed, feeling they're asking too much of you.

- use passive-aggressive behaviors to avoid confrontations.
- express irritation when others insist you get out of your comfortable routines or cozy environment.

Going Deeper

How do you respond when you feel overwhelmed in the presence of people you feel secure with versus those you're less comfortable with?

Which of the average or unhealthy tendencies do you resonate with the most?

Describe a situation where you reacted in the ways described above.

DAY 19

Growth Path

When you believe and trust that God loves you, and all He has is yours, you begin to relax and let go of your personality's constraints and lies. You draw nearer to Him and move in a direction that aligns you with His truth. You feel safe, secure, and loved.

Feeling more joy, peace, and liberation, you stretch yourself toward healthier attributes, even though it is hard. As you grow in faith and depend solely on Him, God blesses you with real and lasting transformation, shaping you into who He made you to be.

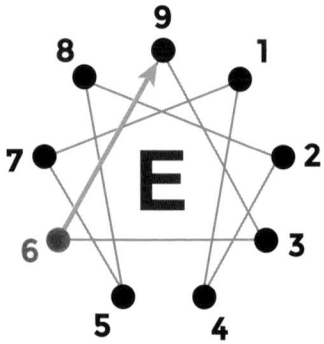

As a Type 6 moving toward the healthy side of Type 9, you can:

- take time to relax and enjoy moments, enabling your mind to slow down.
- empathize with others and extend compassion to them.
- develop secure relationships as you become less reactive, stabler, and calmer.
- grow more open and receptive toward people.
- become emotionally peaceful and self-possessed.

- increase independence by trusting your inner guidance.
- reassure and support others instead of seeking security for yourself.

Going Deeper

When you are growing, what changes about your heart and your typical responses?

_____

_____

_____

_____

_____

Which of these growth attributes would you love to experience more in your life?

_____

_____

_____

_____

What helps to support your growth and flourishing?

How can you incorporate those things into your life more?

TYPE 6 DIRECTION OF **GROWTH**

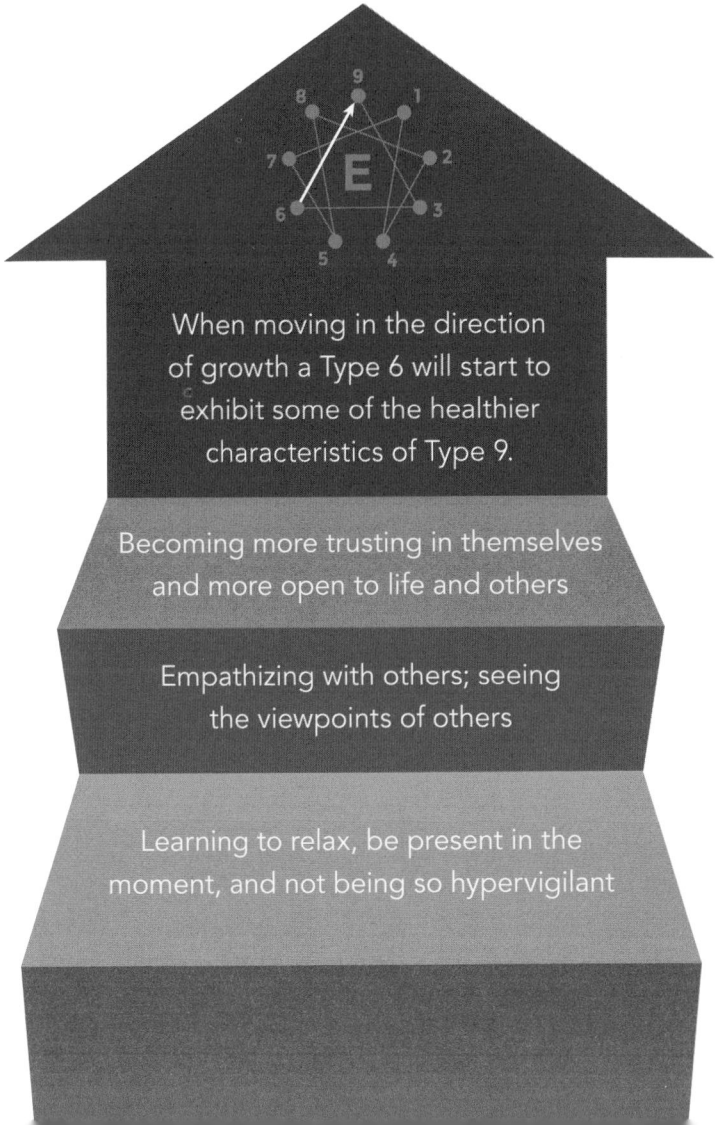

DAY 20

Converging Path

You are your best self on the Converging Path, where three Types come together. Here you access the healthiest qualities of your Main Type, your Growth Path's Type, and your Stress Path's Type. When you live in the fullness of who you really are in Christ, you are freed from the bonds of your personality.

This path of personal transformation can be difficult to reach and maintain. When you first learn about the Converging Path, you may feel it's too hard to travel. But God wants to provide this path for you. Trust Him, follow Him, and ask Him to be with you as you move forward.

As a Type 6 moving toward the healthy side of Type 3, you may:

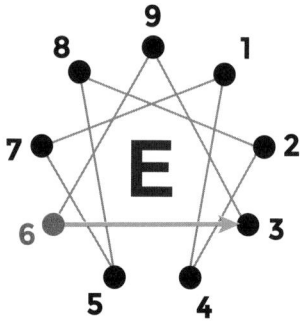

- learn to direct, respect, and trust yourself.
- focus on achievement, taking action to meet your goals.
- devise more effective, efficient, and confident ways to accomplish goals.
- move forward assertively, not allowing your inner committee to sabotage your actions.
- delight in accomplishments, knowing you contributed to something great.
- act bravely for others without getting trapped in worst-case thinking.

Going Deeper

Can you recall a time when you experienced the freedom and joy of the Converging Path?

What was it like when you accessed the healthiest aspects of your Main Type, Growth Path's Type, and Stress Path's Type?

What would help you move toward your Converging Path more often?

Spiritual Renewal

TYPE 6 THE LOYAL GUARDIAN

SELF-PRESERVATION

Grab a journal and write down every catastrophic thought, worst-case scenario, and negative outcome that your inner committee is currently shouting at you. Find a verse of scripture that addresses each of these fears, struggles, or worries, and write them down. Put a line through each item, and reflect on the truth that Christ is your security. He promises to be loyal, faithful, and constant, no matter what lies ahead.

Moving Toward Your Best Self

The journey of exploring your heart is not an easy one, but it's an exciting one.

God has a unique message for each Type. The message He tells you as a Type 6 is: "You are not alone or abandoned."

Yes, you *were* lost, but God knew your great need and sent His Son to rescue you. Christ showed His immense love for you by living a perfect life, dying on a cross for your sins, and rising from the dead to give you eternal life.

When you receive Christ as your Savior, He removes your sins and gives you His perfect righteousness, which brings immediate hope of a bright, freeing, and glorious future with Him. Trust in Him who loves you and went to such great lengths to meet your need.

After you place your trust in Him, you can completely rest in knowing you are not left alone but are intimately known. He cherishes you, provides for you, and protects you. He remains with you always, supplying peace and direction. Fully believing and trusting in Him strengthens your mind and body. You can trust your inner guidance and move forward with confidence.

Each Type has a signature Virtue, which you exhibit when you are at your best, and Type 6's Virtue is *courage*.

When you're courageous, you trust God with your anxieties and insecurities, knowing that He cares for you, even when you face challenges. Believing that God loves you and is good to you lowers your stress and calms your mind. You face life's uncertainties with the assurance that God will always be there for you, meeting your needs for security and guidance.

When you're courageous you also affirm and trust yourself and others, becoming interdependent and cooperative as an equal. Believing in God leads to belief in yourself, which inspires inner direction, positive thinking, willing leadership, and humble confidence.

Using the Enneagram from a biblical perspective can empower you to see yourself with astonishing clarity so you can break free from self-condemnation, fear, and shame by experiencing unconditional love, forgiveness, and freedom. In Him, you are whole. And with Him by your side, you can grow stronger and healthier every day.

Now that you know how to use this internal GPS and its navigational signals, start using it every day. Tune in to how your heart is doing. Avoid your common pitfalls by staying alert to your rumble strips. As you learn new awareness and actions, you will move forward on the path that is healthiest for your personality Type and experience the gift of tremendous personal growth.

Going Deeper

What do you notice about yourself when you're at your best?

What would the world be like without the involvement of healthy Type 6s?

Type 6 VIRTUE

Courage is your virtue.

This allows you to stand up for yourself and others for what is right and good no matter the consequences.

What are some practical ways you can offer your virtue to others today?

Afterword

God's plan to restore the world involves all of us, which is why He made us so vastly different from each other in ways that reflect who He is.

That is why I'm so thrilled you picked up this book and have done the hard, but rewarding, work of looking into your heart. When you align with God's truth, you can support the kingdom, knit people together, and be the best *you* only you can be.

Growth is *not* easy. It requires us to surrender to God, depend on Him, and walk into His calling for us. But when we let go of our control and He takes over, He will satisfy our hearts, filling them with His goodness, and His blessings will flow into our lives and others' lives.

I can attest to God's transformative work having this ripple effect—reaching and positively impacting different parts of our lives and everyone we encounter. As I became more aligned with God's truth (and make no mistake, I'm still in progress!), the changes I was making helped transform my relationships with Jeff, my family, and other people around me. More and more friends, acquaintances, and even strangers were experiencing the transformation that comes from God through the tool of the Enneagram.

I can't wait to look back a year from now, five years from now, or even a decade from now, and hear about the ripple effects *your* transformation has created for hope, wholeness, and freedom. I'm excited about the path of discovery and growth ahead of you! What is God going to do in you with this new understanding of yourself and those around you? What are the things you'll hear Him whisper in your heart that will begin to set you free?

And how will your personal transformation bring positive change to the people in your life?

This is what I hope for you: First, that you will believe and trust in your identity in Christ. In Him, you are forgiven and set free. God delights in having you as His dear child and loves you unconditionally. This reality will radically change everything in you—it is the ultimate transformation from death to life.

Second, I hope that as you discover more about your Enneagram Type, you'll recognize how your personality apart from Christ is running *away* from your Core Fear, running *toward* your Core Desire, *stumbling* over your Core Weakness, and *desperate* to have your Core Longing met. As you become aware of these traits, you can make them the rumble strip alarms that point out what's going on in your heart. Then you can ask the Holy Spirit to help you navigate your inner world and refocus your efforts toward traveling the best path for your personality Type.

Third, I hope that God will reveal to you, both

in knowledge and experience, the transformative work of the Holy Spirit. With Him you can move toward growth, using all the tools of the Enneagram (the Levels of Alignment, the Wings, the Triads, the Enneagram Paths, etc.) to bring out the very best in you, the way God designed you to be. As a result, others will be blessed, God will be glorified, and you will experience the closeness of a Savior who will always meet your every longing and need.

May the love of Christ meet you where you are and pull you closer to God and others. And may you experience the joy of knowing His love for you in a deeper and more meaningful way.

Acknowledgments

My husband: I have to start by thanking my incredible husband, Jeff, who is my biggest cheerleader and supporter. He has helped me use the Enneagram from a biblical perspective and lovingly ensured that I expanded my gifts. Without his encouragement each step of the way, I never would have ventured into this world of writing. Thank you so much, Jeff.

My kids: Nathan and Libby McCord, you are a gift and blessing to me, and an inspiration for the work I do. Thank you for affirming me, being patient with me, and always believing in me. I pray this resource will bless you back as you journey through life.

My family: To my incredible parents, Dr. Bruce and Dana Pfuetze, who have always loved me well and encouraged me to move past difficulties by relying on the Lord. To my dear brother and sister-in-law, Dr. Mark and Mollie Pfuetze, thank you for being a source of support.

My team at Your Enneagram Coach: You enable me to be the best I can be as a leader, and I'm so honored to be a part of our amazing team. Thank you for letting me serve, for showing up every day, and for helping those who want to become more like Christ by using the Enneagram from a biblical perspective. Thank you, Danielle Smith, Traci Lucky, Robert Lewis, Lindsey Castleman, Justin Barbour, and Monica Snyder.

My marketing team, Well Refined Co.: Thank you, Christy Knutson, Jane Butler, JoAnna Brown, and Madison Church.

My agent: Thank you, Bryan Norman, for helping me navigate through all the ins and outs so that this could be the very best work for our readers. Your advice was most beneficial.

My publisher: To Adria Haley and the team at HarperCollins Christian, thank you for allowing me to share my passion for the Enneagram with the world in such a beautiful way through this book collection.

My writing team at StrategicBookCoach.com: Thank you, Danielle Smith, Karen Anderson, and Sharilyn Grayson for helping me create my manuscript.

My friend and advisor: Writing a book is harder than I expected and more rewarding than I could have ever imagined. None of this would have been possible without my most-cherished friend and beloved advisor, Karen Anderson. I am thankful for her heart, her passion, and her help every step of the way. You beautifully take my concepts and make them sing. Thank you!

About the Author

Beth McCord has been using the Enneagram in ministry since 2002 and is a Certified Enneagram Coach. She is the founder and lead content creator of Your Enneagram Coach and cowrote *Becoming Us: Using the Enneagram to Create a Thriving Gospel-Centered Marriage* with her husband, Jeff. Beth has been featured as an Enneagram expert in magazines and podcasts and frequently speaks at live events. She and Jeff have two grown children, Nate and Libby, and live in Franklin, Tennessee, with their blue-eyed Australian Shepherd, Sky.

Continue Your Personal Growth Journey *Just for Type 6!*

Get your Type's in-depth online coaching course that is customized with guide sheets and other helpful insights so you can continue uncovering your personal roadmap to fast-track your growth, overcome obstacles, and live a more fulfilling life with God, others, and yourself.

VISIT YOURENNEAGRAMCOACH.COM/EXPLORING-YOU

The mission of YourEneagramCoach.com is for people to see themselves with astonishing clarity so they can break free from self-condemnation, fear, and shame by knowing and experiencing unconditional love, forgiveness, and freedom in Christ.